Clear-Eyed *Seeker* of Wisdom and Truth

Clear-Eyed Seeker of Wisdom and Truth

Finding Your Way Through The Ideological Minefields

Brian Edmister

XULON PRESS

Xulon Press
2301 Lucien Way #415
Maitland, FL 32751
407.339.4217
www.xulonpress.com

© 2019 by Brian Edmister

All rights reserved solely by the author. The author guarantees all contents are original and do not infringe upon the legal rights of any other person or work. No part of this book may be reproduced in any form without the permission of the author. The views expressed in this book are not necessarily those of the publisher.

Printed in the United States of America.

ISBN-13: 978-1-5456-8011-7

Table of Contents

Great Mysteries 1
Clear-eyed seeker of wisdom and truth – spiders 3
How did Moses get so darned smart? 5
What is missing here? 8
The missing link 10
What about Evolution 13
It's about time 16
What are the odds? 19
What about global warming? 21

Words! 23
Counterfeits 25
Love is the word 27
Knowledge vs ideology 29
Fighting is competing 31
Get a job! 34
Faith, belief and ideology 36
A little about tinkering 38
Thoughts vs feeling – the synthetic environment 41
What about economics? 43
Wealth and Money 45

What does it mean to be educated?............................... 47
Obesity 49
What about "rights?"... 51
What about "Education?" 53

America! The great freedom experiment! 57
Socialism - a capital idea 59
Freedom from religion – please!................................ 62
Noah, what were you thinking? 64
Freedom is a Christian idea...................................... 67
If you are not born with it, you don't have it 70
The frog is boiling... 72
So what's so great about freedom anyway? 75
The politics of anger 78
What does it mean to be rich?................................... 80
We are a Christian nation 83
Parasitic Christians 85
What about poverty?.. 88

Introduction

Several years ago I had the opportunity to teach a Sunday school class for 35-45 year old married couples. I was surprised to learn that many of these people had accepted as truth that "modern science" had conclusively shown that the origins of the world and mankind occurred through a "natural" process and not from any creation process as described in the Genesis account of creation. As a consequence of this belief, they also regarded most of the Bible as mostly fabricated out of embellished stories handed down over many years and, therefore, not reliable as a source for spiritual insight or moral guidance. Yet they felt a need for something higher than themselves, and they came to church regularly and participated in the social functions of the church.

I decided to tackle this acceptance of an ideology which had destroyed their faith in a loving Father who had created them in His image and placed them in a world filled with tangible evidence of His handiwork.

My purpose in this enterprise was to show how to shed one's self from the clutter of these ideas and look clearly at the world and at the reasons why faith in God is not only reasonable but is, in fact, *demanded* by what one sees.

The Genesis account of man's creation has Adam eating of the fruit of the tree of "knowledge of good and evil." While this set in motion man's demise, it also gave man discernment. In any circumstance, therefore, one will always know what the right thing is to do. You may not want to do it, but you will *always know what it is!*

In these short essays on many topics, I intend to not just instruct the reader but I want to motivate the reader to become a clear-eyed seeker of wisdom and truth.

An honest search for truth inevitably leads one to a personal knowledge of the author of all truth. The evidence is stark and overwhelming.

IDEOLOGY: A SUBSTITUTE FOR KNOWLEDGE

When one looks at the way ideas are presented, what is missing from the presentation is often more important than what is presented. For example, when we are told that burning oil for our energy needs has a negative effect upon the environment, the fact that this assertion has never been demonstrated outside of the laboratory is conspicuously absent. It is assumed that the person hearing this assertion is either too young or too ignorant to challenge it. In this way a purely political assertion is fostered upon the unsuspecting person and will likely be assimilated into his thought process as truth. As a follow-up to the ideological assertion, "evidence" is paraded out showing polar bears languishing upon bare rocks, glaciers melting away, sea levels rising and any number of other events that may well have nothing to do with any human activity.

Now it could well be that burning petroleum products in our cars, generating electricity with coal or cooking out on the grill might have some effect upon the atmosphere. The disconnect takes place when no inquiry is made into the motives of the person making the ideological statement. If these statements go unchallenged, they are taught as truth to our unsuspecting children and are incorporated into school textbooks to give the ideas more "official" status.

The end result completely shuts down the investigative process and any disagreement with the ideological conclusion is met with ridicule and anger.

THE ANATOMY OF AN IDEOLOGY

Ideologies are defined by some as just a set of prevailing ideas which are adopted by a culture. While groups of people adopt certain core ideas about man, man's place in society and nature, the origins of things and a host of other ideas, the ideology is inserted into a culture to produce a specific result. These two phenomena are not the same. The one is organic and is open to change, enlightenment and modification, the other is rigid and permits no challenge to its stated conclusions.

Charles Darwin made his now-famous trip aboard the HMS Beagle in the early 1800's. Upon landing in the Galapagos Islands, he noticed several species of what appeared to be finches except that they had developed certain features such as powerful beaks and long slender beaks that enabled them to access food sources such as hard seeds, flower nectar and others. He concluded from this that the isolation of the islands and survival pressures forced a "natural selection" process which caused these features to be expressed over a number of generations. Upon returning to England, he devoted his life to the study of these changes. In his book "On the Origin of Species" Darwin set forth the hypothesis that all living creatures had "evolved" from a common ancestor. His observations were accurate and his conclusions were justified insofar as the variations in this species of finches were concerned. Subsequent DNA analysis of his meticulously preserved specimens revealed that the finches had come from Europe. It remained for others to make the mental leap that "science" had discovered the truth about "creation" and it did not involve a supernatural intervention, but was a completely natural process.

Darwin did not have the benefit of molecular biology or DNA information. In his scheme, the cells were amorphous. Evolutionary complexity and sophistication was a result of more cells. We now know that the living cell is an amazing organism with a complexity that staggers the imagination. We also now know that living creatures do not differ by just a few minor variations in DNA programming, but they differ by billions (or more) such instruction sets. Not only do living creatures differ by a bewildering number of unique characteristics, the integrity of the reproduction process is *very reliable* and randomly induced variations in the genetic code either causes the embryo to die or produces an offspring that cannot survive.

By the beginning of the 20th century, there were intellectuals who were offended by the words in the American constitution that held that man's freedoms were conferred upon him by God. How, they asked, could a god who did not exist confer anything on anybody? Since man, according to the new "scientific" orthodoxy, was just another animal thrown up on the earth like all of the rest of living things, man occupied no favored place in the world. It followed then, according to this "progressive" (or modern) view, that all the rest of the constitutional protections which were derived from the biblical commandments were also baseless. This ideology, which is based upon a flawed assumption about the origins of life, is now widely held by many people and taught as fact to our children. Other ideologies which grew out of thorough-going evolutionary theory such as Marxism, Nazism and Communism have flourished in the 20th century at the cost of millions of lives and institutionalized poverty for many millions more.

IDENTIFYING AN IDEOLOGY

When one embarks upon the career of becoming a clear-eyed seeker of wisdom and truth, the process of navigating around the world of ideas can be very difficult. Everyone on every hand is claiming truth for their position. Politicians who want to be "perfectly clear" are probably peddling some version of an old worn out ideology that will remove your freedoms and your wealth. What are the common features that are earmarks of ideologies?

1. Ideologies are *always* about groups. The individual is always rendered subservient to the group. If you are an African American, you are not a person, but a member of a class. You are expected to behave in a certain way, vote for certain leaders, speak a certain way, raise your children a certain way, etc. If you are a Caucasian person, you may well be regarded as an enemy of an African American and therefore shunned by him.

2. Ideologies *always* need a large number of ignorant poor people who are dependent upon the ideologue for sustenance. Poverty is an essential element in any ideology because successful people have power and will not tolerate having their wealth stripped from them. A large poor and dependent population insures the victory of the ideologue at the ballot box.
3. Ideologies *always* carefully control the content of education offered to your children. Ideological training avoids academic subjects in favor of "social" training. Your children must be taught to be angry at successful people when they grow up without marketable skills. Many of these young people are paid to "protest" against successful people or against companies who disagree with the premises of the ideology.
4. Ideologies *always* attempt to control the institutions of higher learning. Since they are in it for the long haul, it is imperative that future leaders of society be of the "correct" political persuasion. These people will occupy positions in entertainment, social media, government, and education.
5. Ideologies *always* use factoids in their messages. Factoids are words or statements that are outright falsehoods or partial truths that, when repeated many times, enter our vocabulary as accepted truths. They rest upon the "everyone knows" fallacy and are carefully crafted to lead the unsuspecting listener to the ideology's desired conclusions. For example, the word "scientific" is introduced to evolutionary theory to confirm to the listener that any idea of intelligent design is "unscientific" and therefore untrue.

It is very important to remember that you don't have to accept anything at face value. The ideas set forth in our constitution were all based upon protecting the *individual*. There is purposely no mention of groups in the constitution. In this collection of short essays written over a several year period, I attempt to influence the reader to embark upon his own journey to discover the truth about his own life and discover the meaning of his experiences.

Great Mysteries

There are many things lying around in plain sight that are truly mysterious. The natural world is filled with creatures with truly amazing capabilities. In this collection of essays I draw attention to the baffling skills of a tiny spider and the sadly lacking explanation by evolutionary theories to explain how he got them. The "millions of years" explanation just doesn't satisfy simply because spinning a web would have been just as difficult then as it is now. Besides, he would have had to pop up with all of his features intact. No gradual bit-by-bit process could have produced all of his features at the same time. In fact, this is true of all creatures including Man.

Life is clearly a very sophisticated technology about which we know very little.

Clear-Eyed Seeker of Wisdom and Truth

Those of us who earnestly desire to find out the truth of things are assaulted with all sorts of "facts" about everything from religion, to politics, to science and a host of other things that many times do not pass the muster of thoughtful inquiry.

There are many questions that arise in all of these areas that beg for answers.

I would like to see thoughtful answers that anyone might have to some of these questions:

The faith question:

It seems apparent that the human problem with knowledge requires that first we must make a number of faith-based statements about our own existence. For example, the statement that "there is a god" and the statement that "there is no god" are exactly the same from a rational standpoint. That is to say, no evidence can be brought to bear that proves either position. Yet both of these camps zealously guard their own positions to whatever extent they can. If either group has political power, it could actually cost you your life to hold the other position.

As a clear-eyed seeker of wisdom and truth, the circumstantial evidence seems to be heavily on the side of life being a very sophisticated technology which we cannot understand. Where did it come from?

Consider the case of the spider which was hatched inside a box. This spider never saw another spider and never attended seminars on web spinning. He is further disadvantaged in having a brain the size of the point of a pin. Furthermore, as far as we can tell, he doesn't even "know" that he is supposed to survive. Yet he sets about to spin a web to catch a fly he has never seen. In addition, he has two orifices in his small body, one secretes a thick non-sticky web and the other secretes a very fine very sticky web. He spins the non sticky web and attaches it to the floor of the box with the sticky web. He then climbs up the side of the box, hauling the non-sticky web with him, and attaches the other end to side of the box with some of the sticky web. After repeating this process a number of times, he then proceeds to loop the sticky web across the non-sticky strands in close intervals to create the trap for fly he has never seen. He also knows that if he steps into the sticky web he will be caught, He is very careful to walk on the non-sticky web.

The level of highly critical technical choices this little fellow must make to achieve this is staggering. Humans, with all of our brain power, couldn't even replicate the web, let alone create the body that made it.

So I ask: What happened here? It seems that this knowledge must exist somewhere outside the spider and is somehow downloaded when he needs it - including the "knowledge" that he must survive.

How Did Moses Get So Darned Smart?

The first five books of the Judaeo-Christian scriptures are attributed to Moses who lived long after some of the events recorded there. For example, the account of creation found in the early chapters of the book of Genesis, pretty much describes the earth in its early state ('...without form and void."). He then goes on to give a pretty accurate description of the earth as it cooled including the miles thick layer of water vapor that surrounded the planet and prevented any light from reaching the surface ("...and darkness was upon the face of the deep."). As the earth cooled, the water vapor gradually condensed, creating the seas. The light from the sun reached the earth for the first time. ("...and God said let there be light and there was light,..and the evening and the morning were the first day.")

As the water vapor slowly condensed, there was no clear division between the clouds and the surface. The surface temperature of the earth would have been close to the boiling point of water. Volcanoes spewed tons of sulfur dioxide, ash and rock into the newly formed seas, making the water a toxic soup. The next development, according to Moses, was the appearance of a layer of clear air between the surface and the clouds ("...and God divided the waters which were above the earth from those that were on the surface.") The evening and the morning were the second day. How could Moses have known that the air is filled with water?

As the earth cooled, titanic convulsions took place on the new planet that produced rock jutting out above the water as the earth's crust was formed. Moses describes it: "Let the waters be gathered together, and let the dry land appear."

An interesting aside: The next event listed was the creation of plants. The fossil record shows one-celled plants to be the first living creatures to appear. Plants, according to Moses, did not appear in the sea as many scientists assume, but on the newly formed land. This would have been consistent with the fresh water that was abundant on the land from the constant torrential rains. The fresh water made the harboring of life possible. This was the third day.

As the clouds gradually dissipated, the sun, moon and the stars became visible. Moses describes it..." and God made two great lights, the greater to rule the day and the lesser to rule the night, He made the stars also." This was the fourth day.

On the fifth day, God created the birds, fish, mammals, that populated the seas and the land.

On day six, God created man "in his own image." He created male and female and gave them charge over all of the rest of creation.

God rested from his creating on the seventh day.

What does all of this mean?

Moses clearly could not have been there during the millions of years covered in this account. What is so utterly baffling is how he got the general scheme of things right. The fossil record clearly shows a progression of events that closely matches this account, if one assumes that this is how it would have appeared if viewed from the earth.

Now to add to his incredible resume, Moses also came up with a set of guiding principles designed to provide a blueprint for living a healthy, successful and rich life. These principles known as "the ten commandments" stand alone in the history of human thought as the legal bulwark for the most powerful nation in history, These principles have produced the Holy Grail of organized society: fully codified human liberty and justice!

I challenge you, seekers, to set aside your preconceived notion about the world and set down with the most influential book ever to have been written and find out for yourselves.. It's just too easy to dismiss something with which you have never wrestled.

What Is Missing Here?

*O*ver the past 40 years or more, a sure way to get a government grant for research is to propose studying the process by which one species morphs into another. This elusive process lies at the very heart of the credibility of evolutionary theory which claims to account for the bewildering complexity of life that we see on our planet. Yet after countless "studies" costing the taxpayer billions of dollars, this process (if there is one) has never been discovered;

It occurs to me that the reason the process has never been discovered is that there is no process at all and new species arise from a totally different source

It must be noted that species do not differ from each other by subtle variations in the DNA. Rather, they differ by billions of individual instruction sets. A forensic pathologist can quickly determine if a strand of hair is from a gorilla or a human. A complex instruction set for hair exists in all mammals, but none of them are the same. In an evolutionary process by which one species morphed into another, one would expect to find some of the instruction sets to be identical, thus proving that there is a rational bond that definitively binds one species to another.

If there is no process which brought about this incredible diversity of life that we see, what could be the cause? Keep in mind that "absence of evidence is not evidence of absence."

As an observer of living things (including myself) it seems apparent that all living things "know" that they are living and that they must survive. For any "survival-of-the-fittest" scenario to have meaning, creatures must first "know" that they are supposed to survive. If we have tickets to see the Rolling Stones next month, we "know" that, even if we are not *supposed* to survive until next month, we at least know that we *want* to. The birds, mice, lizards, algae, do not have tickets to future enjoyable events, but they, nevertheless, seem to be actively engaged in behavior which will enable them to survive.

One cannot say that this apparent survival "knowledge" could have evolved simply because it would have had to come first. In other words, no purposeful behavior could have come before the purpose.

It seems that life is a result of a pervasive purpose which emanates from some unknown source. This is very troubling to thorough-going evolutionary theorists who have made the leap of faith to the conclusion that all of life arose as a result of "natural" processes, and, even though this process has yet to be identified, the ideology of evolutionary theory is openly taught as fact to our children and acted upon as cultural and moral relativism.

I would like to see a study proposed which has, as its stated goal, to prove the source of this "life force." Funding would likely be slow in coming.

The Missing Link

I saw a statement that made me realize just how committed some scientists are to the theory of evolution as an explanation of how things got here. The Wikipedia entry under evolution characterized it: "...the origin of species by natural selection is one of the most well understood and indisputable scientific principles there is."

There is no question that something has happened over the earth's history which has resulted in the rich diversity of life that we see. Given the complexity of living things, however, there is much room for questions about the process (if there is one) by which this life came to be.

Consider the DNA molecule, for example. The data storage capacity of DNA is absolutely staggering. A child is conceived when two snippets of DNA, half from each parent, come together. The highly sensitive environment in the mother's womb which makes this union possible was already programmed in the DNA of both the father and mother years before this union took place. That very same instruction set is also contained in the baby's newly formed DNA.

A supervisory instruction set is included in the first cell which directs the developing cell to differentiate into the various organs, bones, features, etc. at certain specific times.

Go now thirty years later and multiple trillions (or more) cell divisions and you will find that even the finest nuances of the parental DNA are expressed in the now adult human, even to personality traits, propensities for body weight, vulnerability to some diseases, artistic abilities, interest, and a huge number of other characteristics including hair color, facial features, foot size, etc. All the while, the original cell no longer exists.

Now the theory of evolution by natural selection explanation of how things got here asks one to believe that this level of sophistication is the result of some "natural" process that somehow appeared out of nowhere.

The language of this "scientific" discourse has been so severely defined that no common sense person could hope to understand what is meant. For example, one cannot say that "the robin flies south in the winter in order to escape the cold and snow." That statement implies that the robin had some sort of "knowledge" about the coming winter and the shortage of food. Rather, the statement is changed to say "the robin flies south in the winter and *thereby* avoids the cold winter. Collectively, therefore, only those robins who flew south survived and that behavior is now programmed into their DNA.

Consider the folly of this torture of language: In order for this behavior to have become expressed due to natural selection and survival of the fittest, *that instruction set would have had to have been there first!*

I plead with you seekers. The term "natural" is code name for no-outside-agency in the explanation of how things got here.

Keep in mind that there is *absolutely no evidence* of one species morphing into another. Species differ by *billions* of instruction sets, not just a few as they would have you believe.

What about evolution?

Probably the most provocative idea to come along in the past couple of centuries is the idea that some sort of natural (that is, random) process is at work in the world which accounts for the living things that we are surrounded with.

The frustrating aspect of this is the elusive nature of the process. In spite of many years of study, no clear definition of this process exists. Like religions everywhere, there are a large number of proponents of various views about this, but none seems to have any real credibility.

Some of the troublesome facts that persist to confound proponents of the various theories are:

No matter how far back one goes in the geologic record, no one has discovered any "primitive" or simpler forms of genetic material. DNA seems to have popped up intact at the dawn of life on earth, and, except for the codes on the DNA which produce the diversity of life we see now and historically, it is still the double helix with its staggeringly complex structure and absolutely astounding data storage capacity.

Chlorophyll, another compound necessary for the processing of sunlight and carbon dioxide into food and oxygen in green plants, has also not "evolved" as far as we can tell.

No one denies the complexity and diversity of life forms that are here now. Also, no one can deny that this diversity did not always exist. The farther back one goes in the geologic record, the fewer and simpler are the organisms. The true "smoking gun" of the evolutionary theorist who intends to show that life arose through some sort of random, that is, not outside-directed process, would be the mechanism by which the DNA code morphed over the past millions of years to produce all of the species that we have now. The "mutation" theory put forward falls short of explaining this phenomenon because the number of mutated instruction sets required to produce a new species is not one or two but billions. Much is made of the observation that man shares 95% of his genes with the higher primates. The instruction set contained in the genetic material of man differs by billions of characters, not just a few as is claimed. It is too much of a stretch to think that a single mutation (or even many of them) could have taken place that got all of these data correct at one time.

The true missing link in the evolutionary theory that intends to show that some random process produced all of the creatures we now see is the primary driving force of purpose behind natural selection. Creatures which are "struggling to survive" must first know that they are supposed to survive. By definition, this purpose would have had to *precede* the process. Since purpose seems to be ethereal, it does not seem to be accounted for in this version of evolutionary theory.

We have all seen the highly touted pictures in biology textbooks showing life proceeding from the primordial slime millions of years ago culminating in the Wall Street trader. The problem with this vastly simplified religious statement about man is that modern man did not go through any such process. Man seems to have popped up around 10,000 years ago with his vast intellectual powers intact. In fact, a case could be made that man has *lost* some of his intellectual prowess since ancient man accomplished many things that we cannot duplicate today (like moving 40 ton rocks around with relative ease.)

It's About Time

We use the word time in so many contexts that a whole glossary of meanings would fill a book. In a scientific sense the word time is used to describe and define processes of all kinds. In fact, it could be said that all of science can be reduced to the way we measure time (and its corollary, dimension).

Yet our minds cannot grasp an infinite progression of time (the future) or an infinite regression of time (the past). Since we cannot contemplate the extent of the bubble of time in which we live, we simply pretend that time is finite and we create words to relieve us of the troublesome implications of a universe in which time does not exist. We simply say that something is "zero" if it falls below our sense of importance. Conversely we say that something is "infinite" if it goes on in the other direction. Within these boundaries, we have created a whole structure of certainty. We have assured ourselves with a strong feeling of confidence that we understand the universe in which we live. We have invented a mathematics system which is internally consistent. This system gives us a strong feeling of certainty: we have taken a vote and we all agree that what we think we know is, in fact, the truth about our world.

Stephen Hawking in his book *A Brief History of Time* observes that the only thing we know about time is that it generally seems to move in one direction, from the past into the future. Yet as common sense as this seems, discovering what is the exact present time is elusive because when we try to determine what time it really is, in the cosmic sense, it is already gone. All of our measurements of the cosmos are hopelessly flawed because the phenomena which we observe now happened millions if not billions of years ago and the objects may have disappeared completely.

What does all of this mean?

The Judaeo-Christian scriptures are filled with tantalizing references to how time interacts with mankind. For example, the highly allegorical account of Adam and Eve in the Garden of Eden makes a reference to the "tree of life." The "fruit" of this tree would have taken Adam out of the time domain and would have "lived forever." Consequently, when Adam ate of the "fruit" of the tree of the "knowledge of good and evil," he was told that he would "surely die." The implication here is that Adam, when he ate of the fruit of the tree of knowledge, crossed over into the bubble of time and the process of his eventual death was set in motion.

God, in the Judaeo-Christian scriptures is described as "I am." Other references describe God as "the alpha and the omega, the beginning and the end." Jesus referred to himself as "I am."

Clearly, these characterizations of God have him outside the time domain, as he would have to be if he is, in fact, the great engineer in the sky who invented all of this.

As a clear-eyed seeker of wisdom and truth, there is one absolute truth that cannot be denied: faith is not an option. In order to build any foundation for a reasonable life, we must first decide what we believe. The meaning of our lives is totally determined by what we choose to believe.

It's about time we sat down and wrote down for ourselves what we believe. It is an eye-opening experience.

What are the odds?

One of the most amazing and provocative much overlooked feature of the Judaeo-Christian scriptures is the Genesis creation account. To summarize, there are six "days" of creation that are listed:

1. Day one - the earth is created from a nebulous material. It is described as "without form, and void."
2. Day two - the earth is covered with water and thick clouds. The earth's crust emerges from the water.
3. Day three - First life forms emerge.
4. Day four - Cloud cover dissipates revealing sun, moon, stars. Mammals and diverse land and sea animals appear.
5. Day five - Man appears

There are three very important observations about this:

1. The oldest original manuscripts of the book of Genesis, ascribed to Moses, are very ancient, certainly preceding any knowledge about cosmology, geology, biology, etc
2. Moses was raised by Egyptians, later was a sheep herder, later led the Israelites out of Egypt. Nothing in his resume

seems to reveal any scientific knowledge about astronomy, geology, archaeology, etc.
3. The account of creation found here follows the general scenario of how we think the earth was formed.

But the most amazing feature of this account is that the events are *in the correct order.* What are the odds that a wilderness-wandering sheep herder could have gotten this right? Where did he get this information? The Egyptians were already building pyramids and doing other impossible things when Moses was there. Did they know about it?

Fellow seekers, I would like to see your ideas about this.

Did the Great Engineer in the Sky tell Moses about this when He gave the ten commandments to Moses on mount Horeb? Did ancient aliens visit the earth and tell him? What happened here?

What about global warming?

I have watched the dialogue about global warming (now called climate change) with a great deal of skepticism. My skepticism arises from the solutions that people have put forward to correct it.

The "science" of global warming (and the assignment of human activity as its cause) seems to rely upon a laboratory model which shows that carbon dioxide in large quantities prevents some heat from re-radiating back into space, thus producing a slightly higher temperature on the surface below. Yet carbon dioxide is heavier than air and settles to the surface where it is quickly assimilated by plants and miraculously is changed into food for the plants and oxygen for all living things. Over water the carbon dioxide is mixed with sea water by wave motion and feeds microscopic plant life in the seas. The application of this model to the whole planet is intellectually indefensible because most of the variables are either unknown or not quantifiable.

This short-circuiting of the investigative process to determine if there even is any global warming and that it is connected to human activity is just too easy.

Just suppose that it is eventually proven that the world is heating up and it is definitely our fault. It seems that the correct approach would be a concerted effort to define the mechanism of the process and then find ways to change our methods of power generation, transportation, home heating, etc. to reduce the offending chemicals.

Carbon is said to be the culprit in global warming. Notice here that carbon is lumped together with carbon dioxide. Elemental carbon is relatively inert and simply falls to the surface. Unless it is burned or transformed into carbon dioxide by microorganisms it does not enter the atmosphere at all.

A group of "scientist" (not all atmospheric scientists) who have a political agenda have voted and decided it is our fault that the world is about to overheat. Since (as the logic goes) America consumes the most energy, it follows that we owe the rest of the world for their discomfort.

Taxing Americans is too provincial to be effective. The most flagrant offenders of carbon emissions from electric power generation are China, India, and Russia. Any comprehensive solution to this problem should include every country and should not be via taxation but through technology. American coal-fired power plants are squeaky clean when compared to comparable plants in these other countries.

It seems that we could offer to sell our heat capturing and chemical scrubber technology to these other countries so that they could clean up their emissions.

Much still needs to be done to develop the underlying scientific knowledge about this. So far, what passes for "knowledge" is filtered through a suffocating ideology and has very little or no credibility.

Words

The language of ideologies is filled with words that have been co-opted to mean something other than their traditional and well-understood meanings. Religion, for example, is narrowly defined to mean any reference to God, but faith in theoretical ideologies is permissible in scientific discourse.

All ideologies start with a conclusion. Any thoughtful inquiry is shut down before it even starts and anyone daring to challenge the ideological ideas is met with anger instead of rational conversation.

Counterfeits

It seems that many of us have difficulty discerning the truth from the counterfeit. Our political discourse preys upon this lack of discernment to sell all sorts of "programs" which purport to solve real or imaginary "problems." What has resulted is the huge mess that our country has fallen into both morally and financially.

I have identified several words which are the most-abused:

Faith - This word is used to mean "religion" in popular vernacular. While most religions exercise faith, there are some who contrast faith with "science," implying that science relies on facts, not faith. Therefore science is a superior arbiter of truth and should always be given higher priority in our decision-making process. Consider how the "theory of evolution" and "global warning" are touted as scientific and are taught as fact in our schools.

But a little closer look at the popular theory of evolution, which claims to account for all of what we see around us, reveals a set of faith-based statements that are supposed to be "scientific."

The evolution proponent believes:

"There is no God"

"Everything we see can be explained by "scientific" principles"

"Man is just another animal"

"There is no objective moral standard for man's behavior"

There are a number of other corollaries to these statements, but, in case you haven't noticed, there is absolutely no evidence to support any of these statements. Rather these premises are supported by a number of "scientists" in a voting process and are being forced upon our unsuspecting children by a perverse educational establishment. They rail against "religious" teaching in our schools, all the while flagrantly teaching these religious ideas as "scientific."

The consequence of this "religious" teaching has given us the mess we are in with our education and with our federal financial indebtedness.

In subsequent essays I will talk more about a number of other words like "rich," "poor," "prosperous," "Intelligent," and some others.

What about it, seekers? Can we parse the words and find out what agenda is being promoted?

Love Is the Word

Love! A word that is in such wide use that it defies the imagination to encompass all of its meanings. We use the word to describe a whole array of emotions. We use the word to describe our political agendas (as in "I love the environment."). We use the word to describe how we feel toward other people (as in "I fell in love with her..."). We use the word to describe how we feel toward inanimate objects (as in "I love chocolate.").

Yet when one looks closely at the word, it is used to describe something of ourselves that we think other people might understand. We assume that all people have similar thoughts and feelings and we can connect with people on this subliminal level. Where would the music and entertainment business be without this? It is a universal longing of mankind to love and be loved.

There is a more solid and potent meaning to the word, however, when it describes a principle rather than an emotion. This takes the form of syllogism which generally states: If I love this person, then I will... The action I take in any instance, then, is determined by what I think would truly benefit the person who is the object of my love. In this case, it becomes my personal responsibility to tailor my actions whether they be words or deeds in a way that benefits the person to whom I am directing this action.

When we say we love our fellow man, based on this principle, we want certain things for him: we want him to be free, prosperous, healthy, productive, tall, smart, and good-looking. In short, when we discipline ourselves to make this principle our own guiding principle, we become like a stove: the closer people get to us the warmer they get. Applied to our family, our friends, our community, our nation, what we get is a free, prosperous, just society.

The framers of our constitution apparently had this in mind when they wrote this historic document.

How about it, seekers? Do we have the courage to stand up and take charge of ourselves and take care of the people around us? Do we have the guts to say the word and mean it?

More Counterfeit Words: Knowledge vs. Ideology

I had a conversation recently with a young man about the topic of climate change. I was curious to know what his thoughts were. His response took me by surprise: instead of explaining what he thought about the subject, he launched into speech that escalated into a broad condemnation of society and people who "refused to believe the obvious."

I decided to let it go and started to talk about generalities and his college experience, but he continued on by saying, "you are a pretty smart guy. Why do you not agree with the vast numbers of scientists who have reached the conclusion that man is polluting the world's atmosphere and we all will pay dearly for it?"

My question, I explained, was really directed toward the thought process that brought you to this conclusion. I was not challenging your conclusion, but rather I was curious to know how you got there.

For example, global temperature measurements are controversial by themselves. There is no automatic correlation between these measurements and any particular cause since sun activity, ocean currents; even tidal forces influence the measurements. To correlate these measurements to some types of human activity is a mental leap that short-circuits the clear-eyed inquiry into whether one "believes" this conclusion to be warranted by the facts.

This young man had adopted an ideology put forth by others in lieu of his own investigation. Predictably, his response to questions about the subject was anger at the questioner, not simply an explanation of what led him to the conclusion.

It seems that the adoption of an ideological answer to real or imagined questions about science, social justice, status of life, poverty, and a host of other issues, shuts down the thinking process and leads the proponent of the ideology into a defense posture that initially arises from anger toward those who might question the validity of the conclusions. The unsuspecting and vulnerable student, in this case, had not been taught to parse ideas, but rather was told that these questions had been settled by others more qualified than he, and that anyone who might question the conclusions was just ignorant, and should even be physically attacked or discredited.

What does all of this mean?

Many of our prominent (and publicly funded) learning institutions are now openly promoting ideological answers to the great questions of freedom, justice, private property, right to life, role of government, history, and many others. The inquiry process has been hijacked and replaced with a cookie-cutter set of explanations for every aspect of life.

I urge you, seekers, to teach your children to "test the spirits" and draw their own conclusions based on their own understanding and not accept the first answer that is thrown at them.

Counterfeit Words:
Fighting is competing

One cannot miss the fact that the world seems to be a very angry place. Angry groups are marching everywhere demanding that all sorts of things be removed or changed or at least made "legal." All that is needed to create this anger is the identification of some group that is, in some way, violating the "rights" of some other group. It doesn't matter that no real injury is taking place at all; it is enough that the *perception* of injury is alleged and therefore fighting is called for even including violence against individuals, destruction of property, and even torching of whole communities.

At the heart of this phenomenon is "community organizing." The pitch goes something like this: The "organizer" comes to a neighborhood where social dysfunction and the resulting poverty has destroyed any hope the people might have had. The "organizer" points to large buildings in another part of the city and tells these people that "those people have taken your money." "You must rise up and demand that they give it back. If they resist, you must march in the streets and disrupt their lavish lifestyle which they enjoy at your expense."

The term "political correctness" is the tool by which these organizers create outrage in unsuspecting and vulnerable groups of people. For example, the "proper" response to the shooting of a black man by a white policeman is to take to the streets armed with slogans, provided by the organizers, in enraged "protest." The organizer has successfully caused one group (all black people) to violently confront another group (all policemen). Marauding gangs of these "protesters" now are justified in smashing and burning buildings, killing police officers, and wreaking havoc wherever they go. All the while, the true merits of the incident are not investigated and the violence spreads all around the country via social media.

The PC police have been very busy. We now have "white privilege," where just the shade of your skin is now offensive to some group of people who have a slightly different shade. We have "racists" all around our schools, our government, our communities who are supposedly subverting the fortunes of groups of people. There is a vast conspiracy by some to impose 18th century ideas about God, justice, and private property on poor defenseless people who are forced to live in poverty. These "racists" discriminate against "immigrants who have come to America for a better life.

What does all of this mean?

It is no accident that our children in public schools are not taught to parse ideas about history, philosophical ideas, or social theories. It is not accidental that our children are not taught mathematics or anything about our nation's founding ideas. Instead they are fed a steady diet of PC ideas about race, the environment, "social justice," and a host of other topics including gender and homosexuality. In short, our children are taught to be angry.

Competition, on the other hand, is about a process by which the individual is taught to look inside himself and find ways to make himself stronger, smarter and more able to find rational solutions to the problems he will later face whether it be physical competition or in the arena of ideas. Learning to successfully compete in virtually any arena translates to all other areas of one life. Clearly, fighting does not produce any usable results whatever that would make the individual more able to solve the problems of life.

I beg of you who would be clear-eyed seekers of wisdom and truth. Teach your children the quiet art of competition and you will be giving them the gift of a lifetime.

Get A Job!

The word "job" is another word added to our lexicon of counterfeit words. The word is tossed about by everyone as if they all agreed to its meaning. Politicians are praised if they offer legislation that is supposed to be dedicated to "job creation." Once such legislation is passed, unemployment benefits are extended to give the "jobs" bill time to kick in. In the meantime, the poor jobless person sits around waiting for something to happen. This is a cycle of poverty and will insure that this person stays poor all the while going to the polls and voting to keep the people in power who are the architects of his poverty. After all, everyone knows that we are all "entitled" to well paying jobs, and the "rich" must be compelled to their "fair share" to provide income for everyone else. If you think this process is accidental, you grossly underestimate the sophistication of the process that starts with public education, is actively promoted by entertainment programming on TV, and is actively promoted by so-called "news sources."

What does all of this mean?

If the word "job" is more precisely defined as "employment," it takes on entirely new meaning. Employment is what I do every day to create wealth for others and in the process for myself. If I work for a company, I strive to secure the company's success. I use all of my skills and talents to attract customers to our business and serve them well when they purchase our goods and services. If I am self employed, I work very hard to serve my existing customers well. These people tell others and I develop a reputation for quality and honesty in my own community. When someone needs the kind of service I provide, my name is at the top of the list.

Employment has a much broader meaning when it includes all of the survival skills that I develop for myself: I learn how to maintain my car and my equipment. I learn how to repair my own home. I learn how to keep myself from getting sick. I learn how to paint, till a garden, teach my kids how to do things. In short, I have a very well-paying second job that creates both tangible and intangible wealth for myself. I can *choose* to be employed or unemployed

Looked at this way, it is obvious that a "job" cannot be conferred upon someone by anybody. Payment for non-work deprives the overall society of the wealth which work should produce as well as squanders the wealth of those who have already earned it.

We owe it to ourselves to develop our own skills and talents so that we are valuable to others. In return, we receive payment for our services. Remember, when it comes time for a company to reduce its work force, they never lay off the people who are creating their success.

My question is, seekers, will we choose to be jobless and unemployed or will we get up every morning determined to advance ourselves and the people we serve? Will we *choose* to be employed or wait around for the government to give us some money?

Faith, Belief and Ideology

It's been a while now since I have launched forth into the sea of ideas, but it has occurred to me that their is a lot of confusion regarding what we do and what we think we believe about a whole range of things. We call belief "faith," for example, and then turn around and act in faith about something that originates from our ideology and has nothing whatever to do with what we really believe.

The politician, for example, who encourages voters to support programs that help the "poor" by giving them "free" money, food, cell phones, etc. fully understands that he is taking money from people who have legitimately earned it and is offering it to others who have not earned it. Yet when one examines his personal finances, one finds that he has financial counselors who manage his money so that he has very little or no debt and minimize his tax liability. His money is carefully invested in the very companies he asks voters to hate. He has created and "ideology" which he does not believe and presents it to people as something they should have faith in, at least to the extent that they would vote for him on election day.

Focus now on the individual who is presented with this scheme. His belief system comes largely from the synthetic environment created for him by "news" media, the internet, movies, peer ideas, public school indoctrination. In short, he has spent very little time honing his own personal analytical skills so that he can parse the ideas presented to him. He has received little or no training in his home or in public school that would give him any way to challenge the validity of any ideas at all, let alone ideas that are presented to him in a way that seems to pander to his immediate needs.

If faith can be defined as a motivation for action, it then takes on significance for the individual because it permits him to act in certain way without the tension of questioning the wisdom of his actions. Belief, on the other hand, is based upon a whole collection of impressions, most of which may not be scrutinized at all. Man-made global warming, for example, is taught openly in our public schools as a fact to first grade children. The idea is not challenged in the classroom and the student "believes" it even though the whole scheme arose out of an ideology perpetrated by others to achieve future political goals. The same is true about ideas relating to capitalism, religion. wealth, work skills, reading, math proficiency, freedom, rights, etc.

Without the ability to challenge and test these ideas, the individual is at the mercy of those who would manipulate him for the advancement of their own ideological goals.

Look around, seekers. Have your own kids been taught to parse the ideas presented to them and question the wisdom of placing faith in whatever comes down the road?

A Little About "Tinkering"

Several weeks ago an educator speaking to graduates from a middle school made this astounding statement: "You kids are not exceptional."

What a statement to come from an educator whose job it was to make these kids exceptional!

But he may have been right to the extent that our kids are being betrayed by the very educational system which has been provided "free" by the American public. I wrote a poem several years ago entitled "The Teacher" which puts the finger on what has happened to our educational system:

> The Teacher
> There she was, already old,
> Standing there
> At the crossroads
> Stopping me with her
> Cold blue eyes.
> She terrified me
> In those days
> With her demands
> Always turning my eyes

Outward on the world
Away from the abyss inside
Now I understand her fear.
Late some nights
You will find me there
At that same crossroads
On the chance that
One of mine
Should happen by.

The world is an exciting and wonderful place for children. There are all sorts of gadgets that invite "tinkering" to see how they work. But the teacher and the parent must join in the process of turning their young eyes "outward on the world away from the abyss inside." Modern educational philosophy has set about to validate the "abyss."

Our children are now taught that their "feelings" are good indicators of who they are and what their role in the world is. Children are taught to view themselves through the lens of the "synthetic" environment. They are taught that perceptions of appearance, popularity, sexuality, gender, and many other parameters which are defined by pop culture instruments such as social media, TV shows, school textbooks, are in fact real.

But when a child is taught how to build a kite, catch a fish, build a scooter, roller skate, fix a flat tire on his bike, cook a meal, and a host of other small projects, his eyes turn outward on the world and away from the hopelessness and depression of the social environment promoted by the poverty brokers who now dominate our educational system.

"Tinkering" has produced our most productive people. Not only the famous ones like Thomas Edison, Alexander Graham Bell, Bill Gates, Mark Cuban and many others, but the millions of others who raise much of their own food, make their cars last 15 years, build all of the furniture in their homes (and others as well), keep their homes in tip-top condition, repair porch swings, keep a nice lawn, accumulate wealth through wise frugality, raise wonderful kids who do great things.

My point is, seekers, this may not be rocket science, but it produces rocket scientists instead of the poor lost kids who wind up homeless on the streets of our cities complaining because they have nothing. One of the greatest gifts that you can give to your kids is the rock-solid understanding that they can be successful at whatever they do by thoughtful tinkering.

Thoughts vs. Feelings - The synthetic environment

I wrote earlier about a number of counterfeit words used in our political discourse. The use of the words "thoughts" and "feelings" are used to mean the same thing. Yet thoughts can be analyzed and modified easily by individuals through reading, activities like athletics, acquisition of new skills and self development in areas of interest. Feelings, on the other hand, are largely framed in the context of a person's real or perceived environment. We tend to value ourselves against the backdrop of a whole set of images that have been presented to us from what we are exposed to. The view we have of ourselves is a collage of image comparisons introduced through what we see. If I am short, for example, this conclusion is derived from a comparison of myself to other images of people who are taller than I am, but who seem to be more successful than I at things I value like physical attractiveness, athletic prowess, financial success, etc. Yet these images are synthetically created and have absolutely no basis in reality.

What does all of this mean?

There are two views of every person: the view of myself from inside and the view other people have of me from the outside. Which of the two views is the most reliable? The view from the inside is twisted and distorted and is in a constant state of flux. The view from the outside is relatively constant, but more importantly, can easily be modified by simply associating with different people. If, as a child, I lived with people who were negligent, uncaring and angry, my view of myself was diminished so that I did not have personal self worth. The future was dark and hopeless and I found myself totally unable to be enthusiastic about my life. Learning was next to impossible and I found I was unable to cope with the problems of taking care of myself.

Enter now a person into my life who sees something of great worth in me. This person brushes aside my own perception of myself and imposes his view of the world on me as a place of wonder and opportunity. He enjoys the simple process of living in a way I never saw. I find myself excited about learning, and, most of all, I want to do it for the approval of this person. In the past these people were called *mentors* or *fathers* or *teachers*.

We now live in a culture where mentors like this are very hard to find. The point is, however, we can choose to find these people and associate with them for our own personal success. The synthetic environment created from television, movies, social media, and a host of other fantasy-generated images has left us with no one to live up to.

How about it, seekers? Do we as adults have the courage to be the ones our kids look up to or are we wallowing around in our own self pity?

What about Economics?

There is an economic system that is a natural consequence of our God-given rights described in our Declaration of Independence and defined in our Constitution: It is, in the popular vernacular, called "capitalism."

This economic view of the world of wealth and money derives directly from the view that man is a special creation of a Creator who intended for man to have the dignity of possessing his own "unalienable" rights that do not derive from the largess of a ruling class of people. Among those rights are "life, liberty, and the pursuit of happiness."

If man, then, has this dignity by his birthright, it follows that the wealth he creates belongs exclusively to him and to those he chooses to share it with.

It is this view of man that is under relentless attack by those in our society who seek to get their hands on the wealth created by individuals and use the money to purchase the votes of people who are discouraged from creating wealth for themselves.

While giving lip-service to the "private sector" as being the primary generator of wealth, the secular humanist (code word for those denying the divine rights of individuals) seeks to reach into the lives of individuals and extract an ever-growing portion of private wealth.

It is not surprising that "capitalism" is not taught in our public schools or even in most of our colleges and universities. If man is not a special creation of God, then he doesn't have the right to keep the wealth that he creates.

Our children are being taught that "religion" cannot be mentioned in our public schools. Yet our public schools are actively teaching the religion of humanism (the worship of man) and its natural consequence of the redistribution of individual wealth under the guise of "fairness" and "social justice."

Many of our judges, our legislators and even our president have released a spate of laws and regulations that are specifically designed to strip away the wealth that people create and pour it into the maw of a rogue, corrupt and perverse government.

How about it, seekers? We have a window of opportunity every time an election comes around. If we don't step up to stop these people, there won't be anything left for our children.

Counterfeit: Wealth and Money

The word "wealth" is used so widely that it has largely lost most of its meaning. But the process of creating wealth is at the very core of our constitutionally guaranteed liberties. We have all of these images of the "wealthy" cruising around in expensive cars, eating in fancy restaurants, jetting around the world on expensive vacations. Yet these people do not necessarily have wealth: they just have money. Where they got it, in many cases, is not easily discovered.

I had the opportunity to fly into Israel some time ago and when making the approach into the Tel Av iv airport, the border between Israel and the bordering Arab land was starkly visible. On the Israeli side, the land was green, fish ponds dotted the countryside, orderly homes were built and every inch of land was carefully cultivated. On the Arab side, the land was barren desert with very few signs of cultivation. The same land, same weather, same resources.

Money then comes from the creation of wealth, but it is not wealth. Wealth is created when a person takes the raw material of his own life and turns it into something of value to everyone. Wealth never has finite value: it only becomes finite when it is converted to money.

Consider the young man who decides to take his small parcel of land and see what he can turn it into. He takes a shovel and turns the soil, removing rocks brush and weeds. He finds some manure and spades it into the soil. He plants squash, turnips, beans, potatoes, tomatoes, corn and whatever other vegetables he can find. He waters it and waits. Like a miracle the plants sprout and, in a few weeks, he harvests a bounty of vegetables. These vegetables have universal value and could quickly be turned into money. Stored for the winter, however, they sustain his family in good health. He has created true wealth.

Wealth cannot be "re-distributed." Only money can be re-distributed. When wealth is converted to money and taken from the person who created it, the whole creative process envisioned by our founding fathers is perverted and both the creator of the wealth and the recipient of the money suffer. The creator is discouraged from the creation of further wealth and the recipient is relieved of the necessity of creating anything of value for himself.

How about it, seekers. Are we going to be bamboozled into agreeing to this whole perversion of our language and the theft of what we create?

Counterfeits: What does it mean to be "educated?"

As I have pointed out earlier, the word "education" is used to sell a whole mixed soup of government programs designed to usurp your decisions about teaching and raising your kids. These run the gamut of "teaching" children all about relationships with other children, their parents, their community and the world. The problem with all of this is that no education takes place at all but rather a carefully constructed world view that effectively robs many of our children of the necessary intellectual tools to be financially successful when they become adults.

The process starts out with the teacher. Teacher "qualifications" are carefully designed to require "certifications" by various groups who have, as their main purpose, the promotion of certain philosophical positions. The teacher must prove that he or she has received a thorough training in areas of "sensitivity." These run the range of sexual orientation, race, body weight, bullying, dietary issues, outcome based competition exercises. and a host of other sub-corollaries to these areas. A teacher who can show that he has received all of this training is then said to be "certified" to teach our children. Proficiency in subject material such as math, reading, history, writing, geography, etc., etc. is secondary to "sensitivity" training.

Consider now the 5 year old child who comes to class from a home where there is no father, where English is not spoken, where no home environment exists for the quiet contemplation of ideas, and where he is exposed to neglect and anger. Can the teacher, with all of her "sensitivity" training do anything for this child? Probably not.

There are teachers who mentor their students and make some attempt to give the child the nurturing that he does not get at home. These teachers are heroes, but they will not be able to overcome the influence of the home in most cases.

The definition of education as some level of certifiable training, then, falls short of the true meaning of education which has as its core the acquisition of usable skills and knowledge about the world which equips the student to find a useful niche and to grow up with a constructive attitude about his own life.

Seeker, you must give these things to your children. If you don't they will never become "educated" and may well wind up on the trash heap of life as adults with no hope and no building blocks to become happy and independent. "Life, liberty, and happiness" are our God-given rights, but they must be carefully taught to our children. There are no "certificates" for this process.

Counterfeits: Obesity

Moving along on this series of notes about counterfeit words used in our national discourse, I focus now on the use of the word "obesity." Now people use this word as if it has the same meaning for everyone. For example, the dictionary defines obesity as "In humans, an unhealthy condition caused by gross overweigh; generally any condition where unbridled consumption takes place."

The counterfeit slides in here when "obese" is used to describe "overweight." Arbitrary guidelines have been created by interested groups such as life insurance and health insurance groups to define what a person's "normal weight" is. The fact is, none of these data are statistically connected to whether a person is "healthy." The counterfeit use of "obese" is used by politicians as reason to intrude into people's lives and attempt to dictate what a "healthy" condition is. All sorts of tinkering in this area are being attempted by our current spate of political operatives. Some states (like North Carolina) have actually empowered food inspectors in public schools to open children's lunch boxes under the guise of "protecting" them.

Consider the real meaning of obesity and take a closer look at the practices of our federal government. If there ever was an example of "unbridled consumption" it is the use of our money by our Federal Government. All the while these people rail against obesity in the American population, they pull their swollen bodies up to the public trough day after day and gorge themselves on the lavish luxury afforded to them by our public trust. They travel on the most expensive airplane in the world, stay in the most expensive facilities, feast on gourmet (and unhealthy) foods, hobnob with the most decadent and notorious world figures, and steal billions of our dollars to give to favorite causes (like "green" companies).

How about it, seekers? Can we put these cows on a diet and put our people back to work? Incidentally, work is the only real cure for obesity.

What about "Rights?"

The word "rights" is used everywhere as if everybody knows exactly what it means. Yet this a very important counterfeit that is used to sell all sorts of programs to an unsuspecting public.

The founding fathers intended certain entitlements to be intrinsically attached to *individuals*. These rights are generally described in the Declaration of Independence as "...life, liberty and the pursuit of happiness." They are more specifically defined in the U.S. Constitution in the Bill of Rights and subsequently expanded or clarified in amendments to the Constitution.

The counterfeit of this word creeps in when it is applied to *groups*. It sounds so reasonable to identify the "rights" of statistical groups based on some common characteristics such as race, ethnic orientation, legal status, sexual orientation, gender, etc., etc. So we are told, for example, that we are violating the "rights" of a black man if we object to his ideas, or prefer a definition of marriage that does not include members of the same sex.

"Groups" are said to be "scientific" because researchers identified certain common features of people and gave them a name so that their specific "rights" could be legislated. What has resulted is a bewildering soup of laws and regulations that, in many cases, violate the true constitutional rights of individuals as defined in the

U.S. Constitution. We are told that 25% of prison inmates are black while black people represent only 12% of the U.S. population. This large disparity can only be explained by racial discrimination. Yet if the individual cases are reviewed, there is virtually no evidence to support this conclusion.

The point is that to attain "equal justice before the law" only the individual may be considered. Attaching the person to a group pollutes the legal process and either wrongfully exonerates the individual and/or violates the rights of the innocent members of the civil society who have been the victim of some crime.

How about it, seekers? Do we have the guts to call this by its real name: a gratuitous counterfeit of what our founding fathers intended for us?

What about "Education?"

The mother of all ideas used by our entrenched far-left government to convince people to support a glut of programs for our schools is "education." If you really love your children, as the argument goes, you will support our noble efforts to "educate" them. If you oppose all of the noble ideas, then you do not "love" your children and you should probably be executed.

Yet if you ask most people what they really want for their children, you get an answer that is fairly simple and very do-able:

By the time my children are 25 years old, I want them to be:

1. Doing a job that is meaningful, pays well, and makes a legitimate contribution to society;
2. In a stable marriage;
3. Thin;
3. Willing to help others;
4. Free of any addictive activities (including smoking);
5. Responsible with their money;
6. Increasing their learning by advancing their job proficiencies;
7. Happy.

Yet if these goals are so widely held by a majority of people, why do so many of our children arrive at 25 years of age with almost none of these?

The answer is both simple and very frightening.

For the last 50 years our children have been subjected to a whole host of social and "educational" ideas that fly in the face of our children's success:

1. The whole scheme of taking federal tax money from individuals and then sending a portion of it back to our local schools has given the federal government a strangle hold over what the local schools can teach our children. This reaches into every aspect of learning including the role of parents, the denial of teaching about our cultural roots, the virtual elimination of teaching about our constitution, our founding principles, and our personal responsibility to take care of ourselves.
2. There is an ongoing attack on the institution of marriage. Many federal and state programs that have been created to address poverty have, in fact, promoted the abandonment by fathers of their own children by limiting benefits to mothers who are married.
3. The focus on "social" success essentially robs children of the core goal of financial success and independence. Mark Cuban, the owner of the Dallas Mavericks, was asked when he sold his internet business for $4 billion, "How did it make you feel to be a multi-billionaire?" His answer: "taller and better looking."

What are the answers to all of this?

Jacques Barzun, a Chicago University professor, wrote a book entitled *Teacher in America*. In this book he differentiates between education and training. Education, according to Dr. Barzun, primarily takes place in the home; the schools can only offer training. Education embodies our children's attitudes toward learning and their attitudes toward a whole host of things like work, food, sexual roles, self esteem, etc.

We have succumbed to the temptation of delegating to the government our responsibilities to educate our children, and they have done a terrible job of it.

What about it, seekers? Can we take over the education of our kids and kick the government out of the process?

America – The Great Freedom Experiment

The founding of America upon the principles of God-given freedoms stands alone in the history of mankind. The role of government was crafted to preserve the freedoms of individuals (not groups).

The efforts by some to get rid of the founding principle of freedom set forth in our founding documents reveals the extent to which any mention of God-dependence is hated.

Socialism – A Capital Idea

I have watched the current trend of some calling for Capitalism to be replaced by Socialism. This is a curious development since they are both the same thing. "Capital" is a generic term. It simply refers to an accumulation of resources that is used to create a supply for a perceived need. These resources take many forms and include money, ideas, land, and proprietary technological inventions. Even the intellectual energy to develop the supply of the product or service could be called "capital".

The real issue in this discussion is who should control the capital and the subsequent creation of the product or service: should the government own this process or should the individuals who came up with the idea own the process? In every case, the individual comes up with the idea and then the government co-ops the idea and runs it on behalf of "the people" As a clear-eyed seeker of wisdom and truth, it seems self evident that the government (which, by definition, produces nothing) is ill equipped to initiate the creative process which has resulted in the vast wealth of America. The primary reason this is true is the risk factor, which drives all of wealth creation, is missing from the government's formula. Success is not a requirement for the government in the enterprise. History is littered with the failures of government sponsored enterprises.

In the case of Solyndra, (a manufacturer of solar energy products), for example, the company was formed and supported by millions of government dollars on the premise that solar energy was needed to replace oil as a major energy source since, as everybody knows, oil and coal are wreaking havoc on the environment by causing global warming. While the purpose may well have been noble, the product being made was unreliable, very expensive to produce and not demanded by anybody.

Any capitalist worth his salt would never have invested his capital in such a venture. Yet the government went in and wasted millions of dollars and suffered no consequences whatsoever.

What does all of this mean?

Competition in a free market breeds opportunity for all of the players. It spawns creative ideas, forces efficiency, forces cost reductions, and improves product reliability and features all of which not only benefit the consumer, but also increase the profitability of the investor. *None of these forces exist in a government-run enterprise!*

A perfect example is found in the "universal health care" idea.

The argument goes something like this: All Americans (and probably many non-Americans) should be able to get heath care if they need it. Good health is a right and not a privilege.

One must ask, then, how such a system could be configured to provide such a service. There is unquestionably a demand for health care. Therefore a careful analysis would have to be made as to what this would look like.

The private capitalist would try to devise a way that all participants in the health care would pay for the service. He then would craft a plan which he thinks could be worth the risk. Notice that the capitalist is not factoring the political element in his calculation since it cannot be assessed.

The government, on the other hand, would not factor the cost, but only the prospect that people would have that the need would be filled. The people who were promised "free" services would be encouraged to vote for those politicians promising it. The end result would be that quality health care would gradually disappear altogether.

I urge you, seekers; keeping the nation's capital in private hands is the very best way to insure that our goods and services remain in abundance and of highest quality.

Freedom from Religion? Please!

I recently saw a protest launched against a school principle who dared to pray at a school function. The Freedom From Religion group objected on the basis of a so-called "constitutional" ban on public figures expressing "religious" views in any public forum.

What is the most disingenuous about this is the very idea that any mortal can be "free" from religion.

The term "religion" is loosely applied by such protesters to any reference to God or any other "supernatural" being or entity. The Judaeo-Christian view of man and the world starts with the simple statement: "In the beginning God created the heavens and the earth."

The Freedom from Religion idea is based upon an identical statement: "once upon a time millions of years ago, the heavens and the earth appeared from purely "natural forces." The only difference between these statements is the substitution of "natural forces" for the word "god."

Neither of these statements can be proved. They are both solidly built on a foundation of faith. The one has faith in a creator, the other has faith in an unidentified process which brought about every thing that we see including living things, stars, planets, etc.

Since this is undeniably true, why, then, do these people regard their faith to be superior to any other kind of faith?

The faith in a yet undiscovered process by which everything came to be is, in fact, based on a cultic belief in "science." Scientism (the religion of science) is based upon two assumptions which, briefly stated, go something like: "Since, as we all know, there is no God, something else must have caused the world, universe, life, etc." The second statement is somewhat like the first: "Although "science" has not discovered the process by which all of this came to be, I assume that eventually "scientists will discover it."

Go back now to the protest against this "theist" and try to explain why they think they have a moral superiority upon which to demand him to be silenced.

We cannot know anything with certainty about man, the world, the universe. We are compelled to take a leap of faith in order to go on with our lives.

The choices of what we choose to believe are not superior to one another.

Life, however, seems to be very sophisticated technology about which we know very little. This leads me to lean heavily upon a great engineer in the sky who made it all.

Noah! What Were You Thinking?

Noah, as we all know, talked to God and God told him to build a giant boat. He told Noah that it was going to rain (a novel notion at the time) and that everything was going to be swept away except Noah and his family and all of the animals that were brought aboard the ark.

Consider if Noah were to embark on such a project today.. He would immediately be branded as a wild-eyed crazy man. News stories would be written chronicling the construction of the strange vessel. "Experts" would be sitting around tables discussing whether or not global warming could in fact produce such a rain. Other experts would be wondering if there were environmental "concerns" about the project, especially the impact on the cedar tree population. Protests would be organized to decry the racism and bigotry of not letting anyone other than his family to come aboard the vessel once the rains came. Environmentalists would be horrified at trying to bring mating pairs of animals into the ark, since food and living conditions would be very limited and certainly not very sanitary.

The ark gradually took shape and its size was truly remarkable. Experts questioned whether it would ever float at all. Since Noah did not have certification to pilot such a ship, government agencies sifted through regulations to see if he should be ordered to stop building until adequate studies could be made to determine the seaworthiness of the craft.

Noah's claim that the ark's shape had been given to him from God was met with arrogant smugness since "everyone knows" that the idea of God is quaint fairy tale from long ago that has now been vanquished by "modern " science.

Then it started raining.

The rain came in torrents. Giant subterranean geysers erupted pouring untold millions of water into the oceans and seas. Thousands of people surrounded the ark, trying to get on board. Slowly the giant craft was lifted from the cradles in which it was constructed. It had no engines, no sails, no rudder. It was afloat and now at the mercies of the winds and currents that swirled around it.

Another ark of sorts was constructed a couple of hundred years ago following instructions similar to the ones Noah had received.

This ark, however, dwarfed the original ark and become the giant vessel known as The United States of America. This ark was designed to offer freedom justice and -yes - salvation to a fatally flawed human race.

Just as in Noah's time, the idea that God could speak so profoundly in history was widely ridiculed. So today those who do not understand the deep faith of our founding fathers do not know how the country was founded or, more importantly, why.

The sheer power and majesty of the United States challenges all of these people try to master it, bring it under their control or even dismantle it. They think that they can have all of the freedoms and justice and prosperity while denying the existence of the architect who designed it.

The book of Genesis is required reading for those who would seek to understand what the great creator of the universe has in store for His children If you think this is a fairy tale, I suggest you sit down and write out your own fairy tale. It is an eye-opening experience.

Freedom is A Christian Idea

As I survey the bewildering array of political ideas that float around television, newspapers, social media, overheard conversations, etc. it occurs to me that a point needs to be made to clear the mud out of the water.

There seems to be a general consensus that "religions" are all basically the same. That is, everyone worships the same God by whatever name they give him, and, except for some of the finer theological differences, there is a moral equivalency to the whole religious soup. It follows, then there really is no reason why we can't all "get along." If we could just get past all of the superfluous wrangling about doctrine, we should be able live peaceably together.

Muslims need to get over their idea that everything non-Muslim must be exterminated; Christians need to get over the idea that God somehow has conferred upon them a moral superiority; atheists need to get over there atheism, etc.

A closer look at all of this prompts one to pause over the idea of "freedom." If freedom is defined as being able to think and do what you want, to earn and keep the things that you have created, to move freely around in your own environment, to be safe from harm from other people, to associate (or not) with anyone you wish, and generally decide for yourself what you want to believe - even if the choice sends you to hell, then the fundamental ideas of Christianity are vastly superior to all other theological systems. Even if you do not believe anything about Christian doctrine, the true seeker of wisdom and truth embraces the basic idea of Christian thought because it provides the most sought-after social environment - true institutionally established freedom.

What sets Christianity apart from *all* of the religions of the world is the idea that man is a special creation of God and is endowed with the personal dignity of *deciding his own fate*. Without this basic premise, freedom *is not possible*.

So the true seeker of wisdom and truth who questions everything, with tongue-in-cheek enthusiastically embraces the idea that God created him and, by God, nobody is going to tell him what to do or believe, nobody is going to take away his money or his land or his country, he is going to say what he wants when he wants to, and if anybody doesn't like it, too damned bad!

So when the liberal politician rails against the "intolerance" of Christianity and attempts to stamp it out, what he really is doing is laying the axe at the roots of his own freedom and all others in the society. Totalitarian political systems *cannot tolerate* this individual freedom because free men will not be bullied and have their lives taken over by a bunch of pinheads.

What does all of this mean?

Even if you do not have any faith of any kind in God or creation or moral objectivity, if you are a clear-eyed seeker of wisdom and truth, you must pretend to embrace these ideas and enthusiastically promote them because it is in your own best interest.

What about it, seekers? Have you got the guts to act in your own (and everybody else's) best interest, or will you retreat into the vacant world of an ideology that will ultimately strip you of your dignity and your wealth?

If you are not born with it, you don't have it!

The flurry of political language that surrounds us today is strangely lacking in one important aspect: the primary concept that drives all else in America is that all people are created by a benevolent creator with their personal freedom intact. It is a part of the very nature of man. This idea was the driving force behind the first constitution in human history to fully institutionalize human freedom.

Any thoughtful person will conclude that we must choose what we believe in order to proceed with the actions of our lives. The current "progressive" thought (another name for the age-old humanism of our distant past) has concluded that the Creator referred to in the Declaration of Independence is simply the intellectual trappings of an old outdated and naive society of the 18th century.

"Science" has now shown that man is simply another animal thrown up out of purely "natural" processes. Man does not possess any more rights than any other animal. In fact, many "progressives" believe that the world would be better off without man (or at least many of them).

Lip service is paid to our founding ideas, but the content of most political talk is apologetic about this embarrassing language in our founding documents.

If the reader is a seeker of wisdom and truth, he must conclude that, even if one does not believe in any design or purpose to the world around us, the idea that man is born free is vastly superior to any other premise upon which to build a foundation of laws.

We *are* a Christian nation. We extend legal tolerance to all people of any faith whatsoever *because* we are a Christian nation. You don't have to embrace the Christian faith or any other faith to fully participate in the freedoms of America!

Those who hold all faith-based systems to be "worshiping the same God" should look around. Where in the history of the world has such a juggernaut of wealth and prosperity ever existed before?

I challenge you, seekers, to open your eyes and your minds to what is happening in the world today. Can anyone truly say that any other religious system has produced such prosperity and freedoms for its people?

It is way past time for our leaders to stand up and proudly proclaim the superiority of our founding principles and stop apologizing for the prosperity it has produced

The Frog Is Boiling

We are now well into the fourth generation of people here in America who have been exposed to the low-information teaching goals in our public schools. It should not be surprising to anyone that we now have millions of people who have been taught the following, either overtly or subliminally:

1. There really is no "God" or creator. Science has shown that everything we see around us arose as a result of "natural" forces.
2. Since there is no supernatural origin for mankind, there is no basis for God-given "unalienable" rights to anything, especially life, liberty and the pursuit of happiness. How could a non-existent "God" endow anybody with anything?
3. Our founding fathers, since they based their views about man on this debunked idea that God endowed us all with certain rights, created a constitution which is now out-of-date and quaint, but no longer binding upon our modern "enlightened" society. The phrase "In God We Trust" on our currency is increasingly offensive to many people.
4. Our founding fathers were slaveholders, rich landowners, some fathered children by raping their slaves, they created

a constitution which empowered them to become rich while keeping the poor from escaping their poverty, and a host of other "historical" accusations intended to discredit them in the eyes of our gullible children.
5. The wealth in America created by people somehow belongs to all of us. The rich people got their money by exploiting their employees and overcharging for their goods and services, thus making them richer while everybody else became poorer. These people are to be identified and their wealth stripped from them and "re-distributed" to the "poor."

Yet the idea of personal freedom, which can neither be conferred upon nor denied to anyone, is a *Christian* idea. In order for our freedoms to be stripped from us, we first must be convinced that we never had them. This fundamental premise has now been actively taught to our children by us as parents, by our churches, by our public schools, and our federal government.

A steady drumbeat has been created by all of us who have tolerated this encroachment upon our society. We now tolerate the killing of millions of our babies, the devastation of our economy, the destruction of our homes, the subversion of our children forcing them to grow up with no useful skills or knowledge, resulting in millions of our children living day-to-day on the meager handouts from a bankrupt government, stripped of the dignity of earning their own way.

Are we now so lazy and ignorant that we cannot even see the folly of all of this?

I plead with you, seekers, to start today to rescue your children from all of this. It is easier than you think. Get rid of the outside influences your children have that are robbing them of learning and take charge of that process yourself! We cannot take another whole generation of children who have no direction, no knowledge, and no motivation to be in charge of their own lives.

So What's So Great About Freedom Anyway?

Freedom is hard. You have to get up every day and decide what it is you are going to do. You can choose to do nothing. You can choose to do something to entertain yourself. You can choose to go and work at something. You can choose to save your money, fix your car, paint your house, smoke a joint or a cigarette. In short, you can either choose to build yourself up or tear yourself down. The problem with tearing yourself down is that, sooner or later, you will become dependent upon other people for your livelihood and then they will tell you what to do and you won't be free any more.

The only definition of freedom that has any meaning is simpvly that wherever you are is where you want to be (or at least is heading in that direction). So you have to decide on your own to do things now that you might not like so that in the future you can get to where you want to be.

So what was there about such a simple process that motivated our founding fathers and subsequent generations to sacrifice everything they had (including their lives) to secure freedoms for themselves and their children?

The answer lies in the true nature of man. From the dawn of history, men have been subjugated and enslaved by powerful men who were not accountable to anyone. These men simply took other men's property including their time and spent in upon themselves. Whole populations were enslaved to build monuments to rulers. The men who built the great pyramids had no ownership stake in the finished tomb. We stand in awe today at the things that were accomplished by the pharaohs of Egypt, the Mayan rulers, the Chinese, Alexander the Great, and many others.

These accomplishments pale, however, when compared to the great juggernaut of history known as the United States of America. For the very first time in human history, a nation was founded upon the freedoms of individuals to build and keep the works of their own hands. Never in human history has so much wealth been created with so much benefit to so many people throughout the world.

The United States is standing at a crossroads. One way will take us on into a more glorious and secure future as the power of our people is unleashed. The other way will lead our country into the tyranny of dependence upon some powerful men who will strip us of our freedoms and plunder our wealth for their own pleasures.

A large segment of our population has been convinced that they should give permission to these men to do just that. For a few dollars, a free cell phone, wages without work, and promises that these men will seize the wealth of the "rich" and give it to them, they have enthusiastically supported the very people who will clamp them in chains and get them started building a pyramid to show to history. These are the old worn-out ideas from our primitive past now advocated by "progressive" politicians.

It seems easy now because the plundering has only now just begun. There is still untold wealth that is in the hands of the free people in this country. Efforts are now well underway to coerce people to give up that wealth to a rogue and perverse federal government.

How about it, seekers? Do we have the guts to shut these people down and re-establish our God-given rights to freedom?

The Politics of Anger

For years I have wrestled with the ideas of political liberalism to understand the root philosophical ideas upon which the whole hierarchy is constructed. For some time I looked at atheism as the rational base, but I discovered a number of theological skeptics who were not political liberals. In fact, one fellow who has become a long time friend, said that he was willing to give the founding fathers a lot of credit for basing the constitution upon God-given freedoms because individual freedoms would "not be safe" in the hands of liberal politicians.

I looked at a number of utopian ideas like Plato's *Republic,* Thomas Moore's *Utopia* , Marx's *Das Kapital and* others, but, while these schemes all sacrificed individual freedoms to an all-powerful state, the vocabulary of our current political "progressive" movement does not specifically go back to these sources.

It came to me as I watched the "Occupy Wall Street" people demonstrate against "the rich." These people are *ANGRY*. They are not simply expressing a political idea based upon some set of rational premises. They are simply angry. They are angry enough to kill. They are angry enough to destroy the property of other people. They are angry enough to collectively vote to tear down our constitution and replace it with something else.

Where does this anger come from?

Once I saw liberalism through this lens, many things fell into place. For three generations now, we have watched a revolution take place in our schools and our churches: Our children have been taught that the American Constitution is an old out-of-date document that permits corporations to amass wealth at the expense of everyday working people. As a result, our schools began turning out children who know nothing of our founding principles and who have been taught how to be poor. Yes, we are teaching our children to be poor by teaching them to be angry!

Modern liberal political operatives are now harvesting the results of this process through "community organizing." They go into poor neighborhoods created by their relentless war on the family, their war on corporations, and their war on "poverty" and convince these destitute people that they have a "right" to what others have created. Under the guise of crusading for the "rights of the poor", they bus these people to the polls during elections thus polluting the political system and propelling angry politicians into public office that rob our treasury and destroy our freedoms.

The freedoms we enjoy as Americans are built upon a foundation of a civil society where wealth creation is celebrated. Wealth creation comes from the quiet contemplation of ideas in our homes.

How about it seekers? With each election we have a chance to shut this diabolical process down and create a society where our angry children can become quiet once again and set about to build for themselves a future secured by our liberties.

We may not get another chance if liberalism prevails.

What does it mean to be "rich?"

The word "rich" gets tossed around as if everybody has a good understanding of what it means. To some it means having a lot of money. To some it refers to a nebulous group of people who have stolen money from the poor. To others it is another word for "blessed."

I had the great good fortune to work for one of America's great captains of industry. He had built a relatively small division of a very large company into a major player in the aerospace industry. He told this story to a group of managers in our company:

"We had a large missile contract which was behind schedule, and I decided to go to the facility that was causing the delay and find out what was going on. In the meeting with several of the people in the plant, the machine shop foreman told me the missile guidance module could not be made the way it was designed. In true CEO fashion, I told him if he couldn't do it, I would find somebody that could. He quietly got up from the meeting; left the room got his lunch box and went home. The plant manager sat in stunned silence. I looked around and saw the same look on the rest of the faces at the table."

"I asked around to see where we went from here. Nobody spoke. I started to get an uneasy feeling about George leaving.

The plant manager told me that George probably knew more about the machining of exotic metals and close tolerances than anybody in the industry and was constantly pursued by their competitors."

"I decided it was crow-eating time so I got his address from our files, got into my car and drove to his home. His house was very neat and his lawn was impeccable. I was met at the door by a very pleasant lady who told me George had called and said he was on his way home. She was concerned because she thought he might be ill. She brought me a glass of iced tea and I waited for George to come home. I looked around the room. There were pictures of children everywhere, some with football uniforms, and several trophies on the fireplace mantle."

"As I looked around I had a sudden realization that this man was more successful than I and did not regard me as being superior in spite of my lofty position in our company. I have two sons, but I went to very few of their school activities. They hardly know me. I am treated like a house guest when I come home. All of the millions of dollars that I accumulated meant nothing to them - and they meant nothing to George."

"By the time George returned, I realized that he was in many ways my superior. I apologized for my bad behavior in the meeting and asked him if he would consider coming back and show us what we had to do to fix the problems with the missile."

"He came back. We had a lengthy meeting with the engineers and hammered out a solution that George thought would work."

"I came back to my office a changed man. I had discovered that successful companies are built by building around successful people, and that it means different things to people. Success is like beauty: it is in the eye of the beholder.

"I set about to completely restructure our internal mobility process to build around these successful people and to abandon the traditional promotion scheme based on MBO (Management By Objective), a system designed to convince people that they are not particularly valuable to the company."

My question is, seekers: What about this? Do we have the intelligence to be "rich" like George, or should we spend our energies resenting people like this CEO?

We are a Christian Nation

There is a large amount of confusion about what the phrase "Christian Nation" means. We hear all kinds of rhetoric about America as "melting pot," a "nation of immigrants," a land of "equal opportunity," and many others.

The fact is, all of the features of America that have made it the "shining beacon on a hill" for the rest of the world, derive directly from the underlying premises of Christianity. Whether you believe in God or Christianity or not, these premises are contained in Christianity and the America that we have created based upon these premises cannot exist without them:

The Christian view of man is that man is a special creation of God. God loves all men, not only the ones who profess to be Christians. God wants all men to come to him and worship Him. But God will not coerce anyone; He wants men to come to him willingly. God bestows upon man the dignity of trusting him with decisions about his own eternal destiny. This dignity is succinctly described in our Declaration of Independence..."We hold these truths to be self evident that all men are created equal and are endowed by their creator with certain unalienable rights..." *Christianity alone*, among all of the religions of the world, holds that man is free.

If man is then free, then it follows that he has the rights of free speech, ownership of property, equal justice before the law, etc. as stated in our Federal Constitution. Capitalism is a natural consequence of man's God-given freedom.

We must think twice about throwing out the divine origin of man's rights. Those who advocate this will sadly find out that they have laid the ax at the roots of their own prosperity and the great social adventure that started in 1776 will be destroyed in favor of the old worn-out ideas that have plagued man since the beginning of history.

Parasitic Christians

There is a phenomenon in physics called "parasitic vibrations." If you pluck the string of a guitar, for example, the string next to it vibrates too.

There is no doubt that the founding fathers believed that the foundation for a civil society was firmly established upon the premise that "...all men are created equal, and are endowed by their creator with certain unalienable rights..." Upon this base, they defined the role of government to be the caretaker of those rights. What has resulted from this over the past two hundred plus years is the most remarkable economic and social phenomenon in world history. It was stunningly revolutionary at the time and still is today. The idea that common people collectively making personal choices about their own perceived benefit could be trusted to direct the affairs of the government is still unique in human history.

At the heart of today's debate about the role of government is a powerful challenge to the premise that God even exists and, therefore, certainly did not endow anybody with anything. The people challenging this, however, are living inside of a society created by this premise. All of the natural corollaries that grow out of this premise such as the validity of contracts (including marriage), equal justice before the law, the rule of law, ownership of property (sometimes called capitalism), religious freedom, are claimed by those denying the premise. They believe these things can all be secured for society without the troublesome insertion of God in the formula.

These people are "parasitic Christians" because the dominant culture in the country is still Christian, and the driving force behind the enforcement of these rights still comes from a large majority of the population that thinks their rights are "unalienable." In other words, the proponents of doing away with this limited role of government have an easy time because they are surrounded by people who support the premise, and they are forced to "vibrate" like these people simply because they are close to them.

The proof of this is in their proclamations like "We must always support the rule of law." "Private sector jobs are our first priority." "Everyone has a right to live a life free from poverty." All the while, the laws and directives created by these same people are intended to ignore the role of government as caretaker and redefine it as master.

The truth is that God-endowed rights, whether you believe in God or not, are absolutely essential to the continued prosperity and freedoms that has produced this great country,

The role of government as master is an old worn-out idea that has been tried since the dawn of history with the same predictable results - destruction of wealth, elimination of personal freedoms, institutionalized poverty, social violence, crime, destruction of the home, and the emergence of a ruling class.

This great social experiment called America can only survive if the majority of our citizens have the moral fiber to stand together and defeat this redefinition of what our government is supposed to do.

What about "Poverty?"

Ronald Reagan once said, "People are not poor because they have no money; they have no money because they are poor, and if their poverty cannot be removed, giving them money only adds to their misery." This brought coals of fire from many of the poverty brokers and was blazoned across the headlines for weeks. The sad thing about all of this was that he was exactly right.

We are assaulted with a carefully crafted attempt to sell us all on the idea that wealth should be "redistributed" to achieve a more equitable society and remove the grinding poverty of millions of our citizens. One cannot help but wonder why, after throwing trillions of dollars at so-called "poverty" programs, we have as many or more poor people today than when the "war on poverty" was launched 60 years ago.

The answer lies in a very dark conclusion: totalitarian governments need poor people. When people have their own money, they are powerful and do not need government. These people will not support the redefinition of our government as master in place of its constitutional role as caretaker of our "unalienable" rights.

It should surprise no one that our educational system has been drastically altered so that it produces poor people. Consider the way our public schools "teach" our children:

1. They are given "rights" to privacy, sexual orientation, freedom of speech, freedom from mention of our Christian roots, freedom from learning about our constitution, freedom from learning academic material such as math, English, reading, economics, ethics, objective history, freedom from learning usable skills.

2. Our students are focused upon elements of "social" success such as appearance (including a whole host of curricula associated with race, obesity, sexual orientation, national origin, language, conflict management) and a very determined effort to guard students against any intrusion of ideas that would tend to discredit any portion of these "educational" efforts.

By contrast, a civil society based upon the principles contained in our constitution, not only does not produce poor people via education, but does not need poor people.

By focusing our children from kindergarten through high school in such a way that discourages independence, a large percentage of them will join the ranks of the poor and can be counted on to vote for politicians who promise to take money from working people and give it to them. This is such a universally held educational philosophy in our public schools that one must conclude that it is done by design.

I look at the institutionalized poor rioting on Wall Street and other places against the "rich," and I feel an overpowering sadness for them, because they are powerless to help themselves. It is not surprising that the people who have created this tragedy are now embracing their futile efforts.

The very first order of business in any new order in Washington should be to shut down the whole scheme of funding local schools through federal taxes. This has given a corrupt and perverse federal government a strangle hold over what is taught in our schools.

What about it, seekers? Can anything be done to save our kids from poverty?

This is not the end of the journey to discover the truth about things. There are always new things coming along that shock the senses and *demand* that they be looked at from a set of guiding principles. I urge the reader to set down and draft a copy of your guiding principles. Use these to test the spirits.

"There is a way that seems right unto a man, but the ends thereof are the ways of death." (Proverbs 14:12)

www.ingramcontent.com/pod-product-compliance
Ingram Content Group UK Ltd.
Pitfield, Milton Keynes, MK11 3LW, UK
UKHW022223230426
12048UKWH00016BA/1031